cl🍀verleaf books™

Planet Protectors

Choose to Reuse

Lisa Bullard

Illustrated by Wes Thomas

M MILLBROOK PRESS · MINNEAPOLIS

For Becky & Rachel —L.B.

For all my friends at Ella's Deli —W.T.

Millbrook Press
A division of Lerner Publishing Group, Inc.
241 First Avenue North
Minneapolis, MN 55401 U.S.A.

Website address: www.lernerbooks.com

Main body text set in Slappy Inline 18/28. Typeface provided by T26.

Library of Congress Cataloging-in-Publication Data

Bullard, Lisa.
     Choose to reuse / by Lisa Bullard ; illustrated by Wes Thomas.
         p.   cm. — (Cloverleaf books™—Planet protectors)
     Includes bibliographical references and index.
     ISBN 978-0-7613-6104-6 (lib. bdg. : alk. paper)
     1. Waste minimization—Juvenile literature. 2. Recycling (Waste, etc.)—
Juvenile literature. I. Thomas, Wes, 1972– ill. II. Title.
TD792.B845 2012
363.72'82—dc22   2010053465

Manufactured in the United States of America
1 – BP – 7/15/11

The text of this book is printed on Arbor Plus
paper, which is made with **30 percent recycled
postconsumer waste fibers**. Using paper with
postconsumer waste fibers helps to protect
endangered forests, conserve mature trees,
keep used paper out of landfills, save energy
in the manufacturing process, and reduce
greenhouse gas emissions. The remaining fiber
comes from forestlands that are managed in a
socially and environmentally responsible way, as
certified by independent organizations. Also, the
mills that manufactured this paper purchased
renewable energy to cover its production.

TABLE OF CONTENTS

Chapter One

Think Before You Toss!

Hey, I'm Tyler. See how much trash my family makes? Taking out the trash is my job.

Good thing I've built these **big muscles!**

But all this **trash** isn't just my problem.
It's also really **bad for the Earth.**

Mom agrees that we throw away too many things. So my family is going to **reuse** more. That means using things again.

The more we reuse, the less trash we make.

The trash we all make is usually buried or burned. Someday we will run out of places to bury trash. And burning trash makes the air dirty. Reusing something instead of throwing it away keeps the Earth cleaner.

Chapter Two

No Need for New

Mom and I are going to practice reusing all day. First, we sort out my school supplies.

I can reuse these old pencils when school starts again. They've already been to school, so they're already smart!

Some restaurants give you crayons to use while you wait. If the restaurant isn't going to reuse them, take them for your school supplies.

My big muscles mean my old clothes don't fit. We pack them up for my little cousin. Then Mom takes me to the thrift store. We find great used stuff there.

Instead of throwing shopping bags away, reuse them next time you go shopping. You can also bring cloth bags to the store. You can use them again and again.

Those jeans don't cost much. Maybe Mom will let me get this baseball bat too!

My bike is broken. We drop it off to be fixed. Sure, it would be cool to get a new one.

But getting rid of my old bike would make a lot of trash. **Fixing** it is better for the Earth.

Fixing things is a good way to reuse. The factories where new things are made use lots of power. Using power makes the air dirtier. So remember: new isn't always better!

Chapter Three

Reusing Can Be Fun

We have a picnic lunch with Ben and his mom. We use cloth napkins. That seems really fancy, doesn't it? But we can't reuse paper napkins.

Carry reusable water bottles when you're away from home. Too many plastic water bottles end up in the trash. It also takes energy to make new plastic bottles.

After lunch, Ben and I **trade toys.**

Now we both have **something new** to play with.

Next, Mom and I go to the library. That way, I can build my brain muscle too. I check out two books and a movie for tonight.

Visiting a library is an easy way to reuse. You borrow a book and read it. Then you bring it back so somebody else can borrow it. Library books get reused again and again. Most libraries have music, movies, and video games too.

When we get home, I remember Grandma's birthday. Grandma says homemade presents are the best. I find something I can reuse.

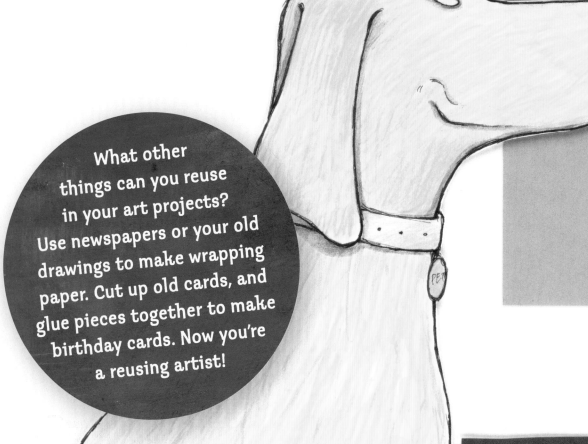

What other things can you reuse in your art projects? Use newspapers or your old drawings to make wrapping paper. Cut up old cards, and glue pieces together to make birthday cards. Now you're a reusing artist!

I'm painting a picture of my dog, Pete, on this can. Now it's a pencil holder for Grandma!

I've been reusing all day long. But too much trash is still being thrown away.

GARAGE SALE →

Will you start reusing too?

Then I can find another way to **save the Earth** tomorrow.

Make Your Own Reusable Napkins

Paper napkins get thrown away after one use. But you can reuse cloth napkins again and again. You can buy fun cloth napkins at thrift stores. Even better, you can make your own cloth napkins by reusing other things.

What you will need:

old T-shirts or an old bed sheet
a 12-inch ruler
a pencil

scissors (Those with jagged edges work best. You can also use a special kind of scissors called pinking shears.)
fabric paint or permanent markers

How to make your napkins:

1) Lay the T-shirt or the sheet flat on a table.

2) You will use your pencil and the ruler to draw your square napkin. Lay the ruler along the bottom edge of the T-shirt or sheet. Draw a line as long as the ruler. This is the bottom of your square.

3) Move the ruler so it is going up from one end of this line. Draw the next line of your square. Draw all four lines until you have a finished square.

4) Ask a grown-up to help with this step so you stay safe! Cut out the square. If you use scissors that have a jagged edge, your napkin will not fray as much.

5) Use fabric paint or permanent markers to decorate each napkin. You can also write the name of a family member on each napkin.

Why not make several napkins for each person in your family? Then you will always have cloth napkins to use even when the dirty ones are in the wash!

GLOSSARY

burned: set on fire

buried: something put in a hole in the ground and then covered with dirt

plastic: something invented by people that can be made into things such as water bottles and toys

reuse: to use something again

thrift store: a place where already-used items are resold

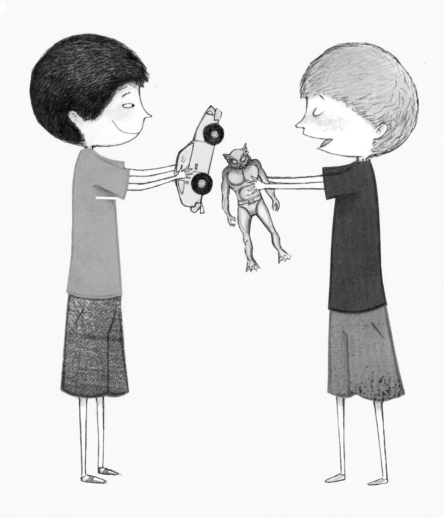

BOOKS

Alter, Anna. *What Can You Do with an Old Red Shoe? A Green Activity Book about Reuse.* New York: Christy Ottaviano Books, 2009. This book has thirteen fun projects you can make from reused items.

Kroll, Steven. *Stuff! Reduce, Reuse, Recycle.* Tarrytown, NY: Marshall Cavendish, 2009. Pinch the pack rat learns how getting rid of some of his stuff can make the world a better place.

WEBSITES

EPA: "Planet Protectors Create Less Waste in the First Place!"
http://www.epa.gov/waste/education/pdfs/jellyjar.pdf
This website from the Environmental Protection Agency lets you download a coloring book showing many different ways you can reuse a jelly jar.

Kids Be Green
http://www.kidsbegreen.org/
Learn about reusing, reducing, and recycling with fun facts, games, and other activities.

One Pretty Thing: "Kids Earth Day Roundup"
http://www.oneprettything.com/?p=3611
See pictures and follow links to many different kids' crafts you can make by reusing.